BRIAN WHITTINGHAM was b   ol at
fifteen he went to work in th   2 he
also attended day-release and   as a
draughtsman, becoming the   design drawing office – the
position he stayed in until 1998. During this time he joined the Paisley
Writers Group and did a number of public readings in places as diverse
as Barlinnie Prison and the Edinburgh Festival, and for three years he
facilitated a new writing group in Maryhill. In 1994 Brian was awarded
a month's fellowship in Yaddo artists' colony in Saratoga Springs, New
York where he co-wrote *Diamonds in Bedlam* with Glasgow songwriter,
Willie Black, which they performed during the *Birth of Impressionism*
Exhibition in Glasgow. He also began writing *Drink the Green Fairy*
whilst at Yaddo. For three years Brian was the East Lothian and
Midlothian Writer-in-Residence, which culminated in *Not So Dusty*, an
anthology of poetry edited by Brian and including some of his poems. He
was also poetry editor on *West Coast* magazine for five years, and more
recently was poetry editor on *Nerve* magazine. In 2002 Brian was com-
missioned by Scotland in Europe to write a one-act play, *The Devil's
Dandruff.*

Presently, Brian Whittingham is working as a part-time lecturer and
tutor of Creative Writing at the Nautical College of Glasgow and has just
completed a three-month Poet-in-Residence post at West Dunbartonshire
Council for Primary and Secondary Schools. He has also been doing
school workshops at Glasgow's Burrell Collection, The Gallery of
Modern Art and The Museum of Transport and is currently working on
children's poetry and new fiction.

Also by Brian Whittingham:

The Old Man from Brooklyn and the Charing Cross Carpet
(Mariscat Press, 2000)
Premier Results with Magi Gibson (Neruda, 1997)
Swiss Watches and The Ballroom Dancer (Taranis Books, 1996)
Ergonomic Workstations and Spinning Teacans (Taranis Books, 1992)

A cunning mix of family memories, traumas of hospital wards, and probing of the relations between art and life. Whittingham brings together with vivid precision and persuasiveness, and some humour, the work of the French Impressionists, the skills of footballers and street entertainers and the difficulty of ironing a seriously crumpled shirt. It is a warm and attractive collection, with a characteristic blend of sympathetic observation and sharp social comment.

EDWIN MORGAN

Brian Whittingham is a poet with a visual artist's eye for the detail of humanity. Like a camera in the hands of a skilled photographer, his poems see, focus on and record the small idiosyncrasies that illuminate his subjects with absolute clarity. In lean, precise words, he captures the fragments others would miss, fragments that reveal us to ourselves in all our misunderstood, tormented and tormenting, half-crazed, wholly human lives. This is poetry that peels away our blindness to the comedy and tragedy of our world and makes us see it with freshly opened eyes. A decade after discovering this poet, I'm still a fan.

JANET PAISLEY

Brian Whittingham's Glasgow is inside him, but it is an adventurous, outward looking Glasgow that travels lightly and with grace. He is rooted in place, but his city is a high vantage point from which to view the wider world. His poetry is not 'nice.' On the contrary this selection contains suspicions, fears, regret, political realities and candour but it has a balance and poise to simultaneously delight in life, and weep over it; with anger and optimism playing to each other's strengths. He is a social poet. A reading of his work has the effect of walking the length of Saucheihall St. or Rue Tivoli. His poems are accessible; appealing in their directness of language and deftness of tone but the accessibility is simply an invitation into somewhere deeper, darker.

CHRIS DOLAN

Drink the Green Fairy

BRIAN WHITTINGHAM

Luath Press Limited

EDINBURGH

www.luath.co.uk

First published 2004

The paper used in this book is recyclable. It is made from
low-chlorine pulps produced in a low-energy, low-emission manner
from renewable forests.

The publisher acknowledges subsidy from

 Scottish **Arts** Council

towards the publication of this volume.

Printed and bound by
DigiSource UK Ltd, Livingston

Typeset in 10.5 point Sabon by
S. Fairgrieve, Edinburgh 0131 658 1763

In memory of
Allan Gerald Whittingham
(my younger brother)

and as always,
for Craig and Debbie,
the constants in my soul.

Some poems in this book have appeared in *Cutting Teeth, West Coast Magazine, Lines Review, Northwards, New Writing Scotland* '13 – Last Things First', '16 – The Glory Signs', '18 – Going up Ben Nevis in a Bubble Car' and '20 – Lunch at Yes', *Back to the Light* [Glasgow Poetry Anthology], *Premier Results, Glasgow Underground Poster,* and *My Mum's a Punk* [Scottish Children's Anthology].

Some of this work was written during a fellowship in 1994 at Yaddo artists' colony in Saratoga Springs, New York – the trip was supported by a travel grant from the Scottish Arts Council. The main body of this work was written during a writing fellowship in East and Midlothian from 1998 to 2001 supported by Lothian Libraries and the Scottish Arts Council.

Contents

CONTENTS

Introduction

I STARTED WRITING WHEN I was 36. At that time, major personal changes were happening to me, then for some reason, I went along to the Paisley writers' group. I reckoned I'd write a few stories maybe. Possibly subconsciously thinking of exorcising certain demons, thinking a little therapy wouldn't go wrong or maybe I was just trying out another artistic fad. I'd already tried the guitar and after murdering Neil Young's 'Heart of Gold' for a couple of years, I turned to oil-painting, learned all the theory about washes and glazing and colour-wheels etc. Next I'd tried out photography till I had F-stops, apertures and shutter-speeds coming out my ears. Then there was the Paisley writers' group. That's when the poetry started.

I'd written nothing creatively before that but had read ferociously since my early years.

Comics during my school-days. *The Hotspur, The Victor, The Valiant, The Eagle, The Beano, The Beezer* etc. My favourite characters were wonderfully real in my imagination, *Jimmy and his Magic Patch, General Jumbo, Bernard Briggs – the Bouncing Goalie, Wilson – the Wonder from Winter Island* and *Alf Tupper – the Tough of the Track,* all weekly visitors inside my head.

And with these comic characters came the annuals at Christmas. The intoxicating *smell* of newness, as if the ink was drying by evaporating into my senses. The *illustrations* that made the characters even larger than my imagination had led me to believe them to be. I could almost see the pages being animated when I read them. This whole experience led to a love affair with books and *The Drumchapel Public Library.*

Novels, newspapers, politics, song lyrics were my fare during my early working years. A teenage head filled with dreams and … *Moby Dick, The Count of Monte-Cristo, Around the World in 80 Days, The Stones, The Who, The Small Faces,* The *Worker's Revolutionary Party, The International Marxist Group*, and a shipyard syntax where expletives and humour were the obligatory stable-mates of lousy conditions that ground down each individual's health that we would all pay for in later years.

Then came years of marriage, family, jobs, unemployment, deaths, separation – all the usual stuff that we have to contend with. Then the Paisley Writers Group. Then Poetry.

The group, Jim Ferguson, Margaret Cook, Graham Fulton, Bobbie

Christie, Ronnie Smith and various others, introducing me to this new enriching experience that was to change my life. Public readings in Barlinne Prison, the Anchor Bar, Heilan Jessies; that was the way of it for these writers who called themselves *The Itinerant Poets*.

That was 16 years ago and I've been writing ever since. This, being my 4th poetry collection that has been achieved with support from many people after the Itinerants, Janet Paisley, Des Dillon, Hamish Whyte, Joe Murray, Kenny McKenzie, Tessa Ransford and so many others who, by their very nature, understand the territory of writing and what it is to have an affinity with language. We never get a chance to thank these people from the being of our souls, maybe the West of Scotland psyche, but deep inside I know how positively they have affected my life, so thanks to you all.

During these years there's been the constant *What is Poetry?* quest that I've had the time to ask many people due to Janet Paisley introducing me to running my first writers' group in Maryhill which has been followed on by numerous groups of all ages and all stages. For me it's sensual imagery mixed with rhythm mixed with that little sprinkle of magic, for others it's something else, but to most people it's something that speaks to our souls and I guess we can't ask for much more than that.

This collection started off its life at Yaddo in 1994, an artists' colony in New York, then it meandered through various phases, the most productive being during a writing fellowship in East and Midlothian, where I worked with and shared the work of many fine people. There are a few stray poems that have found a home here and settled down.

Special thanks go to Willie Black, an outstanding Glasgow songwriter whom I collaborated with on the writing of the *Diamonds in Bedlam* project (Willie wrote and performed some terrific songs) about the French Impressionist painters.

Hopefully, you'll hang some of the poems in this collection in the gallery of your imagination. Possibly, you might even find a few new friends in amongst them.

Toodlypip ...

Brian Whittingham

GLASGOW & LOTHIAN

Glasgow's Inside Me

Glasgow's inside me
like a place name
stamped through a sweet stick of rock.

King William and Bobby Sands
and a bottle shatters against a wall
showering glass splinters
like rainfall on heads of passers-by.

Screeching drag-chain dust-clouds
and cloth-capped
overalled artisans with steel toecaps
cheer at the grimy river's edge.

Young men in young suits
and *talent* done up to the nines
dance round piled handbags
like Indians whooping round a movie campfire.

> The old boy in Kelvingrove Park
> bends, sniffs each rose bush
> to a backdrop of oriental O.A.P.s
> who Tai-Chi in their rising sun.

> The *'Proud to be a Prod'* young team
> banner wave to the tramp
> and whistle of fluted marchers
> trying to remember the past of others.

> The Barra's vegetable slicer's stall
> decorated with carrot palm-tree sculptures
> and the crowd gather closer taken in
> by the Gallowgate merchant of patter.

And like a plant draws nutrition
from the soil in which it grows

Glasgow's inside me
like a place name
stamped through a sweet stick of rock.

Lothian Dusk

A rectangle of sky,
    the top half
    a thick deep red,
    the lower half
    a light blue covered
    by a lemon yellow glaze.

    Superimposed between both
    a triangle of smudged cloud
    showering distant farms.
    The colour & geometry
    of a Lothian evening sky

that if it were in
    an exotic calendar
    filtered to perfection
its authenticity would be considered false.

In Berwick while driving
my passenger and I
remark on this show of nature.

The following day in Port Seton
another described the same sky
    the colours
    the shapes
    the feelings.

And who knows
how many people savoured the scene,
    as if it were their own personal sunset
to be taken home,
tucked into their inside pockets
till the end of their days.

THE SCOTTISH TYROLEAN
YODELLER

The Scottish Tyrolean Yodeller

In the 1950s my mother received
parcelled provisions from her Fatherland.
Clothes and food from my unknown grandparents.

Some days I dressed like a Lüftwaffe pilot
others, a U-Boat commander
and yet others, a Tyrolean yodeller.

School had many problems.

I had the first continental quilt in our street
like a giant's pillow stuffed full of feathers.

I wore the first track-suit in our street
before designers had designs on labels.

I was the only child in our street
to get taken to a delicatessen
and be given a cold braukwurst sausage
to eat on my journey home.

Then, later in the year 2000
I had to empty mum and dad's house
dismantling all that was left of them.

And on checking a drawer
I stumbled upon a letter,
fountain pen writing
in German script I didn't understand
stamped with a Third Reich postmark.

And attached, a studio-posed photograph
of myself as a child
wearing sandals, tartan-hose, dirk, kilt,
sporran, jacket, tartan tie, and Glengarry.

And the blond haired child in the picture
self-consciously
smiled back into watery eyes.

Sewing Fine Velvet

My mother spoke
in her native tongue
when she became excited.

Worked with her embroidery ring
for endless hours.

Would say 'Tschuss'
to departing friends.

I told her
that when I spoke
her language
at school my friends
called me a Nazi bastard
so I didn't
want to learn any more.

She cooked
red cabbage and
mashed potatoes
mixed with cubes of ham

instead of pie chips and beans.

She sat late at night
sewing fine velvet
onto hat frames
that a fat Jew
with a fat cigar
and a smell of
garlic from his breath,
would pay her money for.

She would sing soft foreign songs
when she dusted
and polished
and mended
and cooked

and sometimes mentioned
a *Friedel* or *Pieter*
and a war of loss and shortages.

At Christmas
my mother placed
small decorated bowls of nuts
at the base of the tree
and when I asked
why the cupboards
were always stocked up
with so many tins of food

she would tell me
that you never know
what's round the corner.

Family Ties

Dad asks
if I can thread the wool
through the eye of the needle for him.

He darns his sock
telling me he'd learned how to
with the army in Egypt.
That was when
he joined the bomb disposal squad.

He grins remembering
if they ever came across any bombs
he would have ran a million miles.

We talk
probing each other's past
like strangers discovering.

Dad tells me ...
of a Grandfather in the Lüftwaffe

I remember meeting him
in '74 when I'd hitch-hiked it over.

He was in a hospital bed
blind in one eye
his legacy from a Great War

we couldn't talk each other's language
when we met we just hugged,
I got all misty eyed that day.

... and of a German Grandmother
I never got the chance to meet,
blown up by a British bomb
so the story goes.
Another Grandfather who was
a Newcastle chemist,
'a well paid job in those days'
Dad says

his eyes reflect
another place another time.

and a Grandmother who was
a seamstress from the Big Smoke.

My Brother found her
unmarked grave years later
in Largs cemetery
high on top of a hill with
a white wooden cross
overlooking cold waters.
Little did *he* know.

And as my Dad opens up
about this and that

for some strange reason
I remember the spoon
that was in our cutlery drawer
when I was young.
It had a camp serial number
stamped on it.
It had belonged
to a prisoner of war.

That was in the days
my mother talked to me
in German.

That was in the days
my mother sang '*Que-Sera-Sera*'.

My Grandfather

prepared himself for death
as he would
for an important job of work.

He held it at bay
for months on end
as if it were an ambush
waiting to catch him off guard.

Sometimes
to the background
of ticking clocks
he'd shout at the empty room

    'Ha, now he is coming
    trying to take me
    when I'm not looking!'

My Grandmother
would cover her ears –
move all the ornaments
out of range
of the swinging arc of his walking stick.

    'I'll show him
    who gives orders in this house!' he'd shout.

Always
my Grandfather's final word
on the subject.

Bone China

Filling black bin-bags
with dead dreams
and yesterday's broken hope.

Dad's old kit bag
like the kind slung over shoulders
by sailors
in cinema newsreels.

Mum's musty balls of wool
stabbed with assorted knitting-needles
beside cardigan patterns
with smiling '40s models.

My cardboard silver-foil
21st birthday key,
the chime tinny and out of tune
when I wound it up again
after the in-between years.

The warehouse repayment book
One shilling and sixpence per week
for furniture I can't give away today.

Some things I kept –

The bone-china tea-sets,
willow-pattern filmed with age.

The silver cigarette case
sides dulled
with the tap-tap-tapping
of the ends of plain cigarettes.

And the family photos
of Sunday-best walks in the park.

These things, now join my clutter
until it's someone else's turn to ...

DIAMONDS IN BEDLAM

Introduction

Bedlam (corruption of the word Bethlehem) the popular name for the first insane asylum in England. Built in 1247 as a priory. In 1547 it was officially declared a hospital, exclusively for the insane. As such, it became infamous for the brutality shown to patients. (To this day the word **bedlam** has come to signify any scene of uproar and confusion.)

1876
A press notice on one of the early exhibitions of impressionist paintings

An exhibition has just been opened which allegedly contains paintings. I enter and my horrified eyes behold something terrible. Five or six lunatics, among them a woman, have joined together and exhibited their works. I have seen people rock with laughter in front of these pictures, but my heart bled when I saw them. These would-be artists call themselves revolutionaries, 'Impressionists'. They take a piece of canvas, colour and brush, daub a few patches of paint on it at random, and sign the whole thing with their name. It is a delusion of the same kind as if the inmates of bedlam picked up stones from the wayside and imagined they had found diamonds.

Diamonds in Bedlam
(An appreciation in poems and quotes of lunatics, revolutionaries, would-be artists?)

* *

Absinthe A potent spirit that was popular in the bars, dancehalls, and brothels of Paris. Toulouse-Lautrec was reputed to have a hollowed-out cane that he filled with Absinthe to fortify him when he socialised in the evenings. One of Manet's early works was titled 'The Absinthe Drinker' ... It depicted a cloaked man in shadows, with a glass of Absinthe by his side and an empty bottle lying on the floor. Manet's art teacher was scandalised by the low-life subject matter.

* *

Camille Pissarro ... (1830 – 1903)

His Life in Gentle Colours

The atheist with the biblical beard.

Pissarro's paintings.

A young peasant girl
lying daydreaming.
Poking a stick into
a grassy bank soaked in sunlight.
The dappled greens merging ...
soft blues of her dress.
Creams and reds of her head and feet.

Julie his wife
working in the vegetable patch.
Her back bent
planting seedlings among dull greens.

The femininity of washerwomen
beating their laundry
on a river's rocks.
In the fields
a woman frozen in time,
wrapped against the cold
snapping wood
to kindle a fire's flames
that warm white frost.
And a child holds *her* hands
towards the heat.

And the Louvre
under freshly fallen snow.

Painted during the last winter
of his life in gentle colours.

Soft greys and pinks.
A sense of mid-winter stillness.
And the flick of his paint
the merest suggestion of a barge
on its journey below
on the wintry waters of the Seine.

Pissarro once said ...

The corruptest art is sentimental – that orange-blossom art that makes pale women faint and as for the artist that craves commercial success, I regard it as a waste of time to think only of selling: one forgets one's art and exaggerates one's value.

Edouard Manet ... (1832 – 1883)

Mixing Bold Brush Strokes

Mixing bold brush strokes
with Old Masters'
inspiration
and a feel for modern life.

Manet would repaint
again and again and again
still managing to capture the spontaneity
of his original drawings.

This man about town – this dandy

craved convention
-al recognition
for the unconventional.

His   *Luncheon on the Grass*
            with his nude forgetting
            for the moment
            she should pose
            with the respect of a Greek statue.

His   *Olympia*
            with her prostitute's sexuality
            and erotic adornments.

            An orchid, soft pink in her hair.

            Earrings, Venus pearls.

And a bouquet from an unknown admirer.

and His   *Execution of Maximilian*
with the soldiers' muskets
exploding at point-blank range,
white smoke screens the flames
that extinguish the victim

over a high stone wall
a faceless crowd spectate.

Manet ...

*Every time I paint I throw myself into the water in order to learn to swim but
the attacks of which I have recently been the object have broken the spring
of life in me – People don't realise what it feels like to be constantly insulted.*

Edgar Degas ... (1834 – 1917)

The Painter of Dancers

Studio bound
rendering movement.

Centre-stage
his bodies in space pirouetting,
floating ribbons
pink and blue tutus
twirl, rise and fall,
their ballerina's grace
transformed by footlights.

The orchestra pit,
violins clamped to shoulders
bassoons, oboes,
cheeks swelling, deflating.
The rhythm
of the pounding percussion

and backstage,
the rehearsals,
the repetition,
the continual repetition.
The resting, of exhausted limbs.

Degas –
the painter of dancers
and the fatigue of seamstresses
at the day's end
in their back-street laundry

And the dazed woman
sitting in the grey tavern
with only a glass of Absinthe for company

its sulphurous bright green
reflecting the world pass her by.

Degas ...

*The air we see in the paintings of the Old Masters is never the air we breathe.
The artist does not draw what he sees, but what he has to make others see. The
painter can only do good things when he no longer knows what he is doing.*

Paul Cézanne ... (1839 – 1906)

THE GEOMETRY OF NATURE. Cool tones and flattened stripes. Shapes distorted from various viewpoints. The fundamental plasticity of still-life, cylinders, spheres and cones. Apples and oranges that don't move like people tend to. The difference between reality and a painting. Bold zigzag lines and limestone mountains. Patches of colour and the rhythm of trees, clouds and human bodies, with Cézanne's parallel brushstrokes beneath the surface of life.

Cézanne ...

I should call art, the reproduction of what the senses perceive in nature, seen through the veil of the soul. In art everything is theory, developed and applied in contact with nature.

Claude Monet ... (1840 – 1926)

His Quiet Waters

Monet recorded nature's temperament
as if she were a fickle lover

    Yew Tree
    Clematis
    Iris
    Pansy
    Delphinium
    Jasmine
    Bamboo
    Narcissus

His brushes keeping pace
with scudding clouds
and the sun's flaring light.

    Rose tree
    Azalea
    Tulip
    Aubrietia
    Geranium
    Snowdrop
    Orchid
    Sunflower

Canvases on his easel
rapidly changed.
Slabs of mauve and saffron and crimson

    Alder tree
    Snapdragon
    Poplar
    Hydrangea
    Wisteria
    Nasturtium
    Rhododendron
    Crocus

Slabs of mauve and saffron and crimson
dragged layer upon
layer of time passing
from his dawn to his dusk

    Water lily

the delicate white and rose and yellow
of solitary flowers
dissolving into his quiet waters.

Monet ...

After painting in the open air it was as if a veil has suddenly been torn from my eyes. I understood. I grasped what painting was capable of.

(In 1874 Monet painted a picture titled 'Impression, soleil levant [Impression, sun rising] ... from this painting the title of the Impressionist movement was derisively derived by the critics of the time.)

Pierre-Auguste Renoir ... (1841 – 1919)

A Fullness of Form

Renoir set up his easel
side by side with Claude Monet
to capture the open air.

Painting forests with sparkling rivers
and the light
that would pierce the people and the trees.

Welding their warm reds
and dark blue shadows.
Their yellow orange boats
and bright blue water.

And to express
his pleasure in life,
his rounded nudes.

A fullness of form,
as if they were some splendid fruit
in radiant colour,

      red pimentos
      purple blue aubergines
      yellow green lemons
      and rosy pink plums.

Olive trees and orange blossoms
keeping him company.
And with his paintbrush
tied with ribbons
between his twisted fingers
the old man painted, till the very end.

Renoir ...

I tried long ago to measure out, once and for all, the amount of oil which I put in my colour, I simply could not do it. There is something in painting which cannot be explained, and that something is essential. You come to nature with your theories, and nature knocks them all flat.

Berthe Morisot ... (1841 – 1895)

The Lady who Painted her Life

From the inside out
of her middle-class world

Soft Pastels

Indoors, Julie her daughter.
A golden haired girl
in a green buttoned dress
merges with buff coloured paper.
And friends fix hair,
embroider on wooden hoops
and sit and sew and pose for portraits.

Water-colour washes

Morisot's models ...
Pasie the maid with Julie
and her needlework.
Gabrielle the peasant carries a basin of milk.
Martha the model wears a fur-trimmed coat.
And Morisot's niece and sisters and mother
and lives recorded
sparse as if part of the white paper they were
sketched into.

Sanguine

Outdoors, Eugéne her husband
sits stiff with hands in jacket pockets,
small beard and small bowler-hat.
And Julie with her board-game
on his knees.

Their backdrop of fig, olive, orange and
pepper trees silhouetted against azure skies.

Coloured crayons

The lady who painted her life.
Smudged hues of invisible seclusion.

Mary Cassatt ... (1844 – 1926)

The Solitude of the Lady

At the opera
elegantly dressed
in her black hat, black coat,
and white pearl earrings,
she holds her firmly closed fan.

Commanding her space
on the canvas.
Cassatt's dominant figure
intently gazes through black opera glasses
across the theatre.

The stage lights reflect brightly
on her balcony of gold.

And at the top left hand corner
of the canvas,
a small-scale man
leans from his small-scale box
shared with a smudged woman

and in turn
spies through *his* glasses
upon the solitude of the lady in black.

Cassatt ...

*I doubt if you know what an effort it is to paint! The concentration it requires
to compose your pictures and the difficulty of posing models, of choosing the
colour schemes, of expressing the sentiment ... and oh, the failures when you
have to start all over again.*

Georges Seurat ... (1859 – 1891)

The Serenity of Stillness

In a studio submerged
by books, ideas, theory
and scientific principles
about line and colour and light.

Seurat, would climb
his step-ladder
shutting himself off
from any danger of spontaneity.

Late into his night
he would dab multi-coloured
dots of pure pigment
onto his canvas.

He created his vibration of light
to control the viewer's response.

Formulated lines
and pointillistic patterns
guided his

> cool clarity
> of early morning light

> fashionable Parisians
> walking monkeys

> air heavy
> with mid-summer heat

> circus dancers
> with leaping coat-tails

> Sunday strollers
> strangely silent crowds.

The serenity of stillness.

Seurat ...

Some see poetry in my paintings, I see only science.

Henri de Toulouse-Lautrec ... (1864 – 1901)

Drink the Green Fairy

By day, this pupil of Degas
would draft swift incisive lines
with verve and precision.

In his paintings
he would cut off
bodies and heads and faces at will
and would caricature himself
and others with mockery.

His bold lines
and strong flat colours.

> The white of a Mousseline dress,
> the green of a sash,
> the magenta of a bonnet

would be fixed
by the lithographer's stones
as if spitting printer's ink
onto albums and menus
and theatre-programmes and posters.

And in the evenings,
Count Lautrec would rapidly sketch

his high-class brothels
and prostitutes
with yellow ruffs
and black stockings
perched on red-velvet divans
waiting for custom
under the watchful eye
of their Madame.

And Lautrec shared   their love
                             their vitality
                             their despair
and   their short-lived dreams.

And at *The Moulin Rouge*
he would drink *the green fairy*
and watch *La Melinite*
La Mom Fromage
and *Grille d'Egout*
dance *The Quadrille Naturaliste*

amid gents with black top-hats
and green faced ladies

And *La Goulue* dancing
on bare floorboards
with *The Boneless One*
and marvel at
their passion for movement.

Lautrec ... When offered the LEGION D'HONNEUR
Have you ever thought, Monsieur le Ministre, how strange I should look with the ribbon in my buttonhole when I go to a brothel to paint?

The Moulin Rouge A Parisian nightclub frequented by Lautrec in Montmartre, named after its red mill which was lit up in the evening.

The green fairy Another name for Absinthe, a popular drink in Lautrec's Paris. At 36 Lautrec was to die an alcoholic.

La Melinite & Grille d'Egout Dancers

La Mom Fromage (cheese tart) A girlfriend of La Goulue

The Quadrille Naturaliste A dance that was a form of the cancan

La Goulue (The insatiable) A star dancer at the Moulin Rouge

The Boneless One Valentin, a double jointed male dancer

Vincent Van Gogh ... (1853 – 1890)

The Orphan Man

Alone as an orphan man
in his rough graphite sketches
he painted the internal drama
of the storms in his life,
of the energy in his nature.

Golden-haired wheat
tossed under furious skies
as his mind divorced life's banality.

The angry branches
of poplars, willows
and Prussian Blue cypresses
like the violent flicker of
an extinguishing flame clinging to life.

Vincent, the peasant
who painted and lived
his miners from the Borinage
and peat-cutters
and farmers
and lemon yellow skies
translucent with hope
and ultramarine nights studded with stars
and black crows

hovering over his wheat
ready for harvest.

Van Gogh ...

It is no more easy to find a good picture than it is to find a diamond or a pearl. It means trouble and you risk your life for it. I cannot help it that my paintings do not sell. The time will come when people will see they are worth more than the price of the paint.

It was said that when Van Gogh lived in Arles ...

No one knew him. He lived alone, like a dog. People were afraid of him – he ran around the field with these huge canvases. Boys used to throw stones at him.

Conclusion

An art historian once noted

Van Gogh's greatest love was for the sun, which he glorified in his pictures. Men would have nothing to do with these pictures and laughed at them. And even the sun did not love him; it robbed him of his reason and killed him.

In the last year of his life ... Van Gogh painted a portrait of a Dr. Gachet who was treating him at the time. Van Gogh painted this portrait in the month of June 1890 ... later in July of the same year Van Gogh had taken his own life by shooting himself.
The irony is ... on the 15th May 1990 at Christies in New York ... Dr. Gachet's portrait measuring just 26″ x 22″ was sold for $75,000,000 ... add on commission and a few extras then the bottom line in sterling is in the region of £50,000,000!

... Men would have nothing to do with these pictures and laughed at them ...

I wonder if Van Gogh was up there, his easel in the clouds, painting his beloved sun – having a wee smile to himself?

Impressionists, they take a piece of canvas, colour and brush, daub a few patches of paint on it at random, and sign the whole thing off with their name. It's as if the inmates of Bedlam had found stones by the wayside and imagined they had found diamonds.

An appreciation of lunatics? revolutionaries? would-be artists?

Diamonds in Bedlam

UNKNOWN STARDOM

The Night-Shift Man

He downed a few halfs and half-pints
in the *Seven Seas* public bar.

His night-shift chaser
for the shipyard that never slept.

And inside the fabrication shed
dimly lit
like a Stanley Spencer cathedral,
the half-cut night-shift man,
Lilliputian like
to the QE2's funnels
that almost touched the roof,
he shaped and formed
the cold creaking steel.

And sandwiched in between
showers of spraying sparks
and blinding flashes of light

a deep fill of
rattle hammer clatter screech and whine,

and the night-shift man
played midnight darts,
munched 3a.m. makeshift meals,
and stole forty ... in cardboard box beds.

And when the job went wrong
he '*fucked*' and '*cunted*' and '*whored*'
into the wee small hours.

And in the mornings going home
to his bed he passed
newly risen nine-to-fivers
with faces as dreich
as the clouds above their heads
blotting out the blue of the sky.

The Hospital Chaplain

Ex-Squadron Leader Bradshaw
descends into the ward.
Introduces himself to patients
with his firm RAF handshake.

The wee man puffs his barrel chest.
Smiles his reverential smile.
Mixes his potion
of instant ministerial sincerity.

He pulls up his trouser leg
displaying white scars
on a leg that cannot bend.
Tales of *a* surgeon's scalpel.

Warming to his audience
he tells of how, *his* youngest
is now an RAF flying instructor,
and nearer to God by default.

He recognises ex-Sergeant Murphy,
a face from a past congregation.
Sits on his bed
and softly sings 'We'll meet again' –

they gently sway. Old crooners
giving each other comradeship.
Mock salutes and respect
to years scurrying behind their backs.

– The monitors blip with detached efficiency.

Phil the Fluter

wore burst shoes,
a grey trench-coat,
a trilby that
had seen better days.

He performed
to the shuffling bus queue audience
on his battered taped-up flute.

With 'Stranger on the Shore,'
he serenaded *his* strangers
complete with missing note.
He scuffed past
each potential victim
playing his high speed tune
before the next bus arrived.

To turned heads
he offered his upturned soft felt hat
for recognition never received.

Unknown Stardom

The pot-bellied manager screams

Ah've seen a week in jail pass quicker –
talk tae each other –
yir aw chasin the wan BAW –
Son, yiv goat a heid like a biscuit tin.

The substitutes
keep warm by the touchline,
pass practice balls,
sprint short bursts.

One ball strays towards
a spectator dressed in a suit
who flicks it
from foot – to head – to shoulder – to chest – to foot
and onto the nape of his neck,
like an act from the circus.
He lies face down on the grass
and pushups himself
up and down – up and down – up and down
all the while, the ball balancing.
He stands up,
leans his head forward,
the ball rolls toward his crown
just – as he flicks his head erect
the ball drops into his outstretched hand.

He throws it back to his admirers,
shrugs his shoulders,
buries his hands into jacket pockets.

In this stranger
the boy's eyes
reflect enigmatic dreams
of unknown stardom.

Duffel Coat Dave

Duffel Coat Dave mowed his lawn
bowling green smooth.
Patterned like a football pitch.

Hairdressing scissors
trimmed missed blades
around freshly-painted gnomes.

Duffel Coat Dave swept his path,
his section of the pavement.

Empty milk bottles in his red plastic crate.

He'd polish his patio doors.
Eyeballing the sparkling shine
his face inches from the glass.

He'd re-paint his white-wall tyres.
Minute-wax his bodywork.
Chipped paintwork would be examined
with much rubbing of his fingertip,
much stroking of his chin.

And concealed inside his evergreen bushes
taut piano wire

invisibly protecting the garden's perimeter
from any inquisitive cats
unaware that it was not a good idea
to think about pissing on his lawn.

The Parisian Strongman

The Parisian strongman
wears overalls
over his strongman's hairy chest.

Like gunfire
his whip cracks the air
to extinguish the cigarette
he has placed in a young man's mouth.

He tells his victim
'No need to worry
the hospital is only ten minutes away.'

He clatters Americans on the head
with his caveman's rubber club.
He throws a cannonball
that crashes onto the concrete
then throws a sponge replica
into the crowd
who duck and dive for cover.

The strongman's whiskered face
breaks out
into his showman's grin.

He pulls a beautiful young woman
from the crowd
revealing a giant condom.

The Italians clap and whistle
as he chastises a German
who clunked a few measly francs
into his tin chamber pot,

and as he preyed upon passing women
pinching their bottoms
with wolf whistles and bravado

his lanky assistant
who had sorted out
the escapologist's chains
the juggler's knifes
and the bed of nails

balanced a lethal-looking sabre
on the point of his pointed chin
and strolled about
as if it were the most natural thing
to do.

Sparky's Mother

– has Sparky's pedigree
framed on the wall.
Hand-written in old English.
Centrepiece to prints of her Family.

She mockingly reprimands when
Sparky –   sniffs
              the crotch of the stranger
              who doesn't seem to understand
              how very friendly Sparky can be.

Sparky's mother signs Sparky's name
on birthday cards to her children.
Paw marks drawn in pen.
Crossed bones for doggy kisses.

And when it's Sparky's birthday
Sparky gets to wear an elasticised bow tie
and conical cardboard party hat.

And Sparky's mother kneels on the floor,
holds Sparky's forelegs,
snuggles his golden coat,
and waltzes their doggy waltz
to Sparky's favourite CD.

The Family preparing the cake –
for the – *blowing out of the candles* – routine.

The Vietnam Vet

In the mountains, outside
his *sweat-lodge*
The Vietnam Vet builds a tepee-fire,
snapping
twigs for the framework
that will shelter the fire's core.

He chops logs –
dull thunking;
the measured swing of his axe –
He arranges the kindling
round the miniature tepee,
topping his structure
with dry-grey rocks
that will not spiff or explode.

He ignites frayed hemp,
his bow's cord looped

round a vertical timber dowel;
he rapidly pulls and pushes.

He places the smoky tinder
into the centre of the tepee –
puffing his cheeks –
all the time puffing his cheeks
to keep his flame alive.

He waits –
the ignited timber spits;
crackles its eternal flame.

The woodsman
checks out *his* sweat-lodge

He checks tarps stretched;
tied to bent willow wands
he has formed and bound
into a small dome shaped hut –

tugging the ties – making sure.

The Woodsman returns to his fire
shielding his face –
and with a gloved hand
he tongs the home-made coals,
clunking them into his bucket.

He carries his load;
places his bucket inside
the lodge's centre pit.

Stepping outside,
the Woodsman strips off –

re-enters the *lodge*,
crouches like a hunter.
Makes certain
all exits are sealed

He sits on scattered fern –
in the lodge's darkness
the rock's faint glow.

He scoops cups of water
dashes them onto
the hot rocks;
A loud hiss – a mist of white
hot vapour fills the hut;
curls around his body.

This steam – this breath
of the great spirit
opens the pores of the mind –

His purification.
He closes his eyes,
crosses his legs;
rests each hand gently
on each knee

the steam settles
slowly – sweat trickles.

The Woodsman meditates –
like the *Sioux* before him
who cleansed
themselves of all human scent;
who purified
body and soul;
who sang
sacred-songs –

in their sweat-lodges
with their willow wands
clad in buffalo skins –
so long ago.

On being a Clerk

Tom was a fat man
tall and a bald head with beady eyes
he would rotate
in different directions at the same time
while saying
'I look at things this way!'

In the factory office
he'd play shoulder charges
hopping on one foot with arms folded
and maiming any clerk crazy enough
to challenge him, the more wily opponents
swerving before impact
allowing Tom to crash into the metal lockers.

At lunchtime he'd play chess
six challengers at a time looking
like mimics of Rodin's *Thinker*
wearing their brown dust-coats
with chessboards set up on desks and chairs and filing cabinets

and as they attacked his Sicilian defence
he countered playing speed chess
moving like *Billy Whizz*
checking and mating
leaving the brains of the department
feeling as if they had
had another intellectual *boot in the balls.*

At Home with Lightnin' Hopkins

Playing his weekly floor-spot,
The old guy hunched
with his back to the audience,
clutching his harp
to the microphone.

The resident band's lead singer
walked the dog.

The keyboard player
grimaced to his bouncing keys
as if about to lose control.

The guitarist lazily played bottleneck
with a baseball cap and drawl,
ideal for selling evening newspapers.
And if he was moved by the blues
he kept it all to himself.

And when the applause subsided
the old guy retired
to the bar,
unwrapped his teeth from his hanky,
placed them in his mouth.

Said he couldn't play
with his teeth in,
said he'd learned his trade
playing at home with Lightnin' Hopkins.

He wrapped his harmonica
in his hanky.

Placing the makeshift parcel
in his pocket,
smiled a young man's smile.

For all the Ladies in the House

The purple-lit stage
swirls smoke machine mist.

Five soul-brothers in velvet suits
boogie onstage,
arms out-stretched like tilted aeroplanes
they flicker funky fingers.

The lead singer
informs the ladies in the house, that he

'*Ain't too proud to beg*'
as he lets the mike stand fall forward
and, at a precise moment
stomps on its base,
it catapults back into his waiting hand
on cue, he gets on down, on one knee,
telling the ladies in the house
'*I-wanna-keep-you-any-way-ah-can*'
and with perfect timing
the brothers loosen their velvet bow ties
and throw them to the floor.
The main man sings
to the ladies in the balcony,
with his hand on his broken heart, he's

wishing it would rain
so the raindrops will hide his teardrops

and the crowd go crazy
feeling the feeling
of the joy of being sad again,
the joy of being
young again just
remembering the feeling – just.

(In 2001 The Temptations played the Glasgow Pavilion to a full house and standing ovations. They formed in 1961.)

A Few Swallies

In the Oil-Rig inspection department
the men wore green overalls, yellow hard hats,
carried clipboards and measuring tapes.

In their office
they smoked pipes as if
it were a Sherlock Holmes convention.

The new man –
had recently been promoted
from the shop floor
and found the monthly wage
impossible to manage.

He'd sit, surrounded by reports,
theodolites and dumpy levels
and, the week before payday –

in amongst the smoky figures
he'd scoop up papers in both hands
throwing them into the air
like confetti at a wedding.

'I'm surrounded by complete incompetents',
he'd shout at no-one,
crashing his fists on the desktop.

The other men carried on puffing their pipes,
recognising it *was* the end of the month,
and things would look better for the new man
in the club at dinner time
after he'd had a few swallies of the *gabby-watter*.

64

This Vicky-Bar Elvis

The resident guitarist.
A spattering of well-oiled regulars.

Both – over-familiar
with evenings lost
in the communal oblivion
of cover songs and alcohol.

Barstaff dry glasses.
Crumple crisp bags.

Then – as an in-betweeny
the singer half heartedly mimics
the **King** and his *Suspicious Mind*

A wee man in the corner, curls his lip,
leaps from his chair.

Centre stage he gives it laldy
shoogling his legs,
pointing his arm above his head,
thrusting his groin into his *Jailhouse Rock*

A barmaid leaps from the bar
and jives amongst the tables.

The small audience
bop – cheer – stomp.

And the wee man grows
into his gold lamé jump-suit,
blue suede shoes,
jet black hair and dark shades.

And, for a golden moment
this Vicky-bar Elvis
embroiders his magic-spell
into the fabric of our lives' ordinariness.

Alma and the Bald Man

Alma the embalmer
is a fattish woman
who wildly waves
her hands in the air
as the DJ shouts *'shake yir shammy!'*

is a fattish woman
whose tattoo of a red devil
with its wicked smile on her breast
peeks from her low-cut dress

is a fattish woman
who sits with her crossed legs encouraging
her short black sequinned skirt
to become suitably shorter

is a fattish woman
who drinks
brandy and babycham
in extremely large volumes

is a fattish woman
who gives the men she wants
her black plastic business card
when she has them
  ... over to hers.

And between false-nailed fingers
her cigarette's glow pierces
the club's red, blue and yellow spotlights
bouncing from the ceiling
diffusing on

a man with a purple blazer
and a bald head
fuelled with whisky and bravado
who unwittingly prepares himself
to become her latest beau

the latest love of her life
when he pushes against her groin.

Her womanly charms and cheap perfume
seduce his manhood
during the smoochy number
that is a *'ladies' and gents' choice.'*

Alma whispers to the bald man
telling him of the vibrator she received
as a keep in touch gift
from her ex who still worships the ground etc.

And, holding each other
ever so tightly
before the club's houselights
are once again switched on

Alma and the bald man
dance their one night stand.

The Remaining Pieces of Val

One night Val danced her slow dance
with one hand on the man's hip
and the other held gently in the air.

She told him that was how she danced
with men she met for the first time.

And at the end of the slow dance sequence
he asked if she cared
to meet sometime for a drink
or whatever?

She replied
she would consider lunch.

She always got to know her men
by doing lunch first
she told him.

She suggested
over a brandy and babycham
they could make arrangements
then proceeded to drone on
about her Tenerife singles' holiday
and her peeling sunburn
on her shoulders and boobs.

He noticed how she said the word *boobs*
and how she called the other dancers
chaps and *gentlemen.*

She told him how she had been separated
for three years
but her husband still wanted
to come round and cut her grass.

He must love you very much, he thought,
as they danced the last dance
forgetting about her hand-holding rule.

He helped her on with her coat
and asked her back to his for coffee

and in the early hours, they *did lunch*
and the next day when he noticed
the sunburned flakes on the carpet
the remaining pieces of Val were hoovered up.

Cutting it with Billy the Looker

16 years old
we sampled under age beers
in the only pub that served us
no questions.

Billy who looked
like a cigarette-card footballer
always
lumbered the lookers.

I on the other hand, well
I had convinced myself
the secret of success
lay in the barbershop illustration

and to fix my shortcoming

I visited Fuscos the Italian hairdresser
for a style of the moment
fixed by a mist of Cossack hair-spray.

That Saturday yet again on the sniff
in our black raincoats
that for once
served a practical purpose
as it pissed down from the heavens

and as we headed for the dancing

I glanced to admire my hair-style
in a shop window
satisfied not a hair had been misplaced

until I noticed
the side-effect of the hair-spray & water mixture
was that I could chap my hair
with my knuckled hand
and hear a hollow sound
as if
a rigid shell had been fixed to my head.

In those days
trying to cut it with *Billy the Looker*
was no easy matter.

Crumpled Shirt

This shirt lies on the ironing board
like it's the *creased shirt*
Heavyweight Champion of the World.

It tries to psyche me out
mockingly challenging me
to land the first blow.

I'm in quick –
iron setting MAX
auto 20g steam
skooshing spray like a man possessed.

I'm relentless,
the bit with the buttons
the back
the bit with the buttonholes
the sleeves
the collar …
I stand back exhausted

then I notice this shirt smirks
and when I examine it closer
I see the creases are still there,
not so pronounced this time, more subtle,
but nevertheless still there.

It's then I realise this shirt
has once again defended its crown
and any talk of a re-match at this juncture
would be foolish on my part.

Maybe it's time I thought about hanging up my iron.
Maybe take up another career
where crumpled shirts are
obligatory.

The Three Sisters

We ramble a rock-strewn trail
deep into
the mountain's shaded hollow
leaning like cartoon characters
into the wind.

My middle-age steps
trail behind
my daughter's childlike energy.

I periodically pause
for a breather
and she patiently joins me
and wonders at the dots of cars
crawling below on the tiny road
scratched into the mountain's base.

I remark
the clouds wrapped round the shoulders
of the Three Sisters
look like mufflers against the shifting wind

and my daughter
points out, that to her
the clouds are like giants leaning over
the mountain-tops
slumbering after their day's journey.

And the Three Sisters
impassively ignore us,
content with
the serenity of their Glen.

WILD TIGERS OF
BANDHAVGARH

The Clay Tiger

I'm a clay tiger, woman-made.
I'm muscle and blood.

I'm an earth-brown-red
as if the colour of my heart
has become the whole of me.

I'm surrounded by watercolour brothers
hiding in their artist's jungles.

I have no bones man can use
        to grind into tonic
                that he thinks cures his head-ache.
I have no whiskers man can use
        to boil into lotion
                that he thinks cures his tooth-ache.
I have no flesh man can use
        to bubble into medicine
                that he thinks cures his belly-ache.

So, for the moment I'm safe,
still, always on my guard.

See how I'm ready
crouching
poised, prepared to pounce, if required,
on *the* most dangerous of animals

– mankind.

(Inspired by a plaster sculpture [titled – 'Muscle and Blood'] by Nicola Hicks,
exhibited in the *Wild Tigers of Bandhavgarh* exhibition at the Burrell
Collection during the year 2000.)

The Watercolour Tiger

When peacocks-blue call
through green jungle vine.

When white cattle and black ibis doze.

When slithery snakes slide
through the undergrowth.

When white-plumed egrets wing to roost.

When chitals first bark
from distant dusky mountains.

When women
with yellow, blue and purple saris
with full baskets balanced on their heads
walk home the dusty road, graceful as deer.

When the rays of the large orange sun
like evening fingers
tuck in the little sleepy village.

The tiger wearing
his orange black-striped coat,
peers through
the brown, green and gold
of his tall-grass bamboo curtain

with orange watching eyes.

His ears alert, twitching.
His sharp teeth bared.

(Inspired by an egg tempera on paper painting [titled – 'A Watching Eye'] by
Lars Jonsson, exhibited in the *Wild Tigers of Bandhavgarh* exhibition at the
Burrell during the year 2000.)

The Wire-Mesh Tiger

Its wire-mesh tail in a frozen flick.
It bares wire-mesh teeth,
roars a silent roar

and when the museum's
thick oak doors creak shut
and keys clunk in their locks,
when lights are dimmed
and workers button up to the night

the wire-mesh tiger creaks to life
pads paw-prints
on the carpeted walkway,
feels the cold
of the red sandstone floor

peers through the windowed wall,
under stained glass paintings of
dragons, saints and angels
towards the slumber of Pollok Park.

Cosy in their fields
Highland cattle in long-hair blankets
snuggle on a brown-leaf bed

beside chestnuts knocked to the ground
by playtime daytime children.

The wire mesh-tiger
yawns a wire-mesh yawn
then beds down for *his* night
in an oak four-poster bed.

The wire-mesh tiger
dreams of home and brothers and sisters
in the baking sun and swishing trees.

In the morning's early hours
a bird song alarm
tears the tiger from his dreams.

And as the rays of the fresh sun
sparkle through
a stained glass angel

the wire-mesh tiger of Bandhavgarh
once more resumes his frozen pose,
preparing for visitors of the new day.

(Inspired by a galvanised wire sculpture [titled – 'Bandhavgarh Tiger'] by
Kendra Haste, exhibited in the *Wild Tigers of Bandhavgarh* exhibition at the
Burrell during the year 2000.)

NACHO-MUNCHERS
& DOLLY-GRIPS

Looking for Business?

At midnight on Christmas eve
in mid-stride
automatically
she repaints her red lipstick lips
as she runs across the road.

Clacking heels on black.

An unseen driver
rolls down his window,
his engine purrs to a halt
in the dark street covered with
night-frost and ever so thin ice.
And, with her short suede skirt
and shiny black bag,
she tips her head
towards the stranger in the car.

Topped and Toed

'Topped and toed'
that was how she put it,
'I like a man to be
topped and toed,' she said.

He asked her to explain
where she was coming from.

'His hair must be smart
and his shoes
must have a quality shine,
if a man is topped and toed
then you know
he looks after himself
and if he looks after himself ... welllll'

and as he asked her
'what about the bit in-between?'

she'd already begun the business
of looking for a man
that would fit the bill.

The Beating Heart

The beating heart   will not   read a good book
                                       snuggle under covers
                                       whisper goodnight

The beating heart   will not   wipe sleep from bleary eyes
                                       stretch early morning limbs
                                       wash tiredness away

The beating heart knows nothing of   seconds, minutes, hours
                                       dawn or dusk
                                       birthdays celebrated

The beating heart knows nothing of   laughter of the soul –
                                       being broken in two –
                                          these tricks
                                          played by the mind.

The beating heart has no respite.

It beats its own time   until the day.

Jollies and Junkets

In the library – the librarian
in the empty untraceable office
researches obscure books
and when footsteps approach,
nervous shuffling and the clicking off of lights.

In the surgery – the GP
does some letters,
her euphemism for stretching out fast asleep
horizontal on the examination couch
ideal for 40 winks behind closed doors.

In the newspaper office – the journalist
is working from home.
He leaves his phone off the hook
and periodically phones in to touch base
in between the pub, a round of golf, or whatever?

And in years gone by,
In the shipyard – the nightshift welder
jumped the wall for a few pints,
studied form in the cludgie,
put his line on with the store-man bookie

and because he reckoned
with their jollies and junkets
the bosses paying the wages
were the biggest skivers of all time

on Fridays he would
swallow cans of lager lovelies
while sitting on his porcelain throne.

The Unexpected Visitor

The patient was tired
of form-filling questions
from clipboard inquisitors

tired of the flicking of veins
and jabbing of needles
and filling of syringes with blood samples
for the nurse nick-named Countess Dracula

tired of clusters of white-coats
flipping files, poking fingers
and cold listening stethoscopes

tired of needled drips
tired of popped pills

so he put on his dressing gown
and visited

the man in the next bed
connected to
electrodes suckered to his chest
and resting his head
on puffed pillows.

This unexpected visitor
sucked on grapes, asking
'Did they say when you were getting out?'
'What like's the food?'
and other standard
hospital-visitor questions.

'It's a beautiful day out there,' he said
standing up and looking out the window
at the view
the man lying down could only imagine.

The unexpected visitor checked his watch,
'Better go,' he smiled.

He wandered back to his bed
and tied his cover in giant knots.
'That'll give old crabbit features something to girn about,'
he said as he ticked off
semolina and prunes on the evening menu.

Liar, Liar, Pants on Fire

She applied prebase
as a primer
to even out her complexion.

She applied concealer
to light-enhance
the inner corners of her eyes.

She applied foundation
powder
blended over her face.

She applied eye shadow
brushed through her brows
to give definition.

She applied highlighter
sweeping over
brow-bone and lid for radiance.

She applied terracotta
over her moving eyelid
to complement her green eyes.

And after curling her eyelashes

she applied lash-lengthening mascara
allowing the lashes
to dry between coats.

She applied cream blusher
blended onto the apples of her cheeks
for a healthy glow.

She applied orangey-brown lipstick
followed by
clear lip gloss.

She put in her contacts

tonged curls
into dyed hair
fixed with heated rollers
sprayed with lacquer.

She varnished nails,
sprayed a mask of perfume,
slipped on high-heels,
put on her coat with padded shoulders.

Her once open door
slamming behind her.

He felt suspicious
that all was not as it seemed
when he sniffed
the fragrance in the air
she left behind.

Love isn't – Love is

Love isn't
a high-priced diamond ring
that glitters like fool's gold
on the finger of the prospector
drunk with delirium of perceived wealth.

Love isn't forever
honey-bunch darling smoochy-coochy-coo
or other sweet nothings
that disappear into the air
like wedding confetti lost to the wind.

> Love is
> sharing the stirring of your soul
> with a friend,
> who travels on their journey
> or arrives at their journey's end.

An Eternal Flame Flickers

Napoleon's *Arc De Triomphe*
with the names of Generals
and battles long gone –
chiselled into its concrete legs.

Old men
support a fading flag,
blow a bugle,
rattle a snare drum.

And one looking like the leader
he no doubt was,
wrapped in a grey raincoat
with his red beret
and white armband,
shakes hands with each comrade
showing due respect
with not a word
passing between them.

Tourists
modern voyeurs,
as one by one
the old men disappear
into a door in the *Arc's* leg.

An eternal flame flickers
beside flowers
trimmed in red, white and blue
on the brass plaque
of the tomb
of the unknown soldier.

Darkness descends
along the *Champs Elysées*

a street café silently sits –

Vacant tables and chairs
anticipate the summer
crowds to come.

91

Coronary Care

On Christmas day

the nurses
cover a makeshift table
with a paper towel tablecloth.

The white-gowned
patients from various wards
introduce themselves to each other.

The nurses pour sparkling wine,
tune in to a radio's Christmas cheer,
give everyone a paper party-hat.

> Frank, who's been told
> he's a 50/50 chance with his forthcoming bypass
> smiles and jokes like there's no tomorrow.

> James, who'd had a balloon inserted
> in an artery, slowly raises his leg into the air
> telling all, the doctor used helium by mistake.

> Francis, with her Christmas eve attack
> tells everyone, the last time she'd had red roses
> was when she'd had her *first*, 30 years before.

The nurses, like magicians
lift the aluminium lids off the plates
revealing the steamed turkey dinners

and as glasses are raised for a toast –
outside the window
a seagull lands on the rim of a chimney pot
and momentarily peers into the ward.

A Reading of Form

The Scottish poet

reads his Scottishy poems,
written in a form he understands
is essential.

'NOT – self-gratifying *free verse*.'
He smirks a smidgen – knowingly
when articulating the words –
'*free verse*'

He reads each poem in Scots.
Then English.
Then Scots.

His minister-like voice
soothing

his congregation
sitting on the book-shop floor
leaning against shelves
nursing book-launch – red or white,
still as stiff hardbacks.

His flock
nod their heads knowingly
as he stresses
the significance of syllable count,
with all the solemnity
his minister-like voice can muster.

The Eighth Wonder of the World

Top-hats, tails, evening gowns.
Hyped-up expectations
eager to catch a glimpse
of the eighth wonder of the world.

To capture the first photographs of Kong,
the boys from the press jostle.

Cameras fix the subject's growing agitation.
Flashbulbs explode blasts of light.

Out of control
the *press* press forward
as Kong snaps free of his chains
charging his captors
who scream in all directions.

He trashes skyscrapers,
snacks passing trains,
spits out limbs of rag-doll victims.

He climbs the Empire-State
his soul torn to shreds
and his love for Fay Wray intact.

He pounds his chest with an unheard roar.

As biplanes riddle Kong with bullets
he fingers the patches
of warm wet blood
he cannot understand.

The Paparazzi below
record his final fall.
Lenses hungry for their latest tit-bit.

'The airplanes done it,' the police chief
reminds us in the final reel.

'No, it wasn't the airplanes,' says Carl Denham,
'It was beauty that killed the beast.'

Time Stands Still

Blackpool's north pier.
Worn slats creak.
Wrought iron railings crusted
thick white paint.
Holiday-makers
shorts and beer-bellies
licking pink/white ice-cream.

    Sea-gulls squawk
    perch on tannoy speakers
    listen to George Formby's
    'with me li'l stick o' Blackpool Rock.'

The 'Sandcastle Typhoon Lagoon'
its hooter honking
the countdown for the wave machine.
Bathers like lemmings preparing.
  Stalls.
      Choco-fruit lollies.
      Multi-coloured glass tower replicas.
      Sticks and sticks and sticks of striped rock.

Promenade air scented
with fish n chips n mushy peas
with 1/2 pound mega-burgers
with fried onions spitting spattering
bare armed chefs.

    A Blackpool picture postcard
    showing the old man with beery nose
    at the hotel entrance
    telling the young bride to
    come in out of the rain
    as she looks as if
    she could do with something warm
    inside her.

Small cheap plastic men who pish
when their heads are pressed down.

    Side-shows that guarantee prizes
    for all women and children.

Tramcars shoogle their golden mile.
Brylcreemed conductors
diligently snib and unsnib
their tram doors at every stop.

    And the Tower Ballroom.
    Glass chandeliers drip
    from carved ceilings.
    Ornate golden balconies.

Centre stage Ray McVey.
His tartan jacket.
His Wurlitzer.
His red velvet curtains.

    Sparsely seated holidaymakers
    Bitter – 99p a pint.

The ballroom dance floor.
The afternoon couple waltzing
the woman with perfect posture
perfect grace
bonded at her toes and hands
to her partner
with his wig and loads of class

    And instead of their slacks
    and holiday shirts,
    it is easy to imagine
    her in a shimmering gown and
    him in bow-tie and tails
    gliding and pirouetting
    and whirling frantically

as if
Blackpool's time stands still.

Rush Hour

At the bus stop
the rain drums its thudding rhythm
off the black of their umbrellas.

They jostle for position
peering into an impenetrable jungle
of double-deck buses.

They press and shove,
check watches
with glances as heavy as the sky.

      Then, like an orderly conga line,
      Hare-Krishna devotees
      wearing sandals and robes,
      thread their way
      through the un-noticing crowd.

      They chink
      delicate horizontal cymbals,
      chant words of
      spiritual guidance.

      They tell the world
      'Say – Gouranga – be happy.'

The 32 for Carnwadric
halts too early,
throwing the queuing crowd into disarray.

It's then the mob surge forward.

Yet another Bride

The young French tutor.
A naive arrival who alights
from the black coach with spooked horses
and the strange-looking coachman
with a face as friendly as a freshly-nailed coffin.

And when the Mademoiselle
creaks open the Inn's oak door
amidst the revelry of chattering
serving wenches and clacking tankards

she asks for directions to the count's castle.

Sudden silence cloaks the company
as they view the stranger with knowing fear
putting on their coats leaving
half-eaten meals and hurriedly departing
crossing themselves.

And the timid inn-keeper and his wife
exchange knowing glances of terror
as he rapidly bolts doors, latches windows
shutting out the shadow of the fortress
on the black mountain-side.

The moon vanishes
under cover of cloud
as unseen wolves howl despair.

The virgin arrival looks on
with a puzzled expression not understanding
her scripted potential
to become yet another bride.

The Glen of Weeping

In the Glencoe visitors' centre
tourists in shorts and backpacks
troop into the tiny video theatre.

From speakers a Scottish folk-singer
tells of the popular myth
of MacDonalds murdered by Campbells.

The video footage rolls
with cardboard cut-out clansmen
fronting winter stills
of the *Glen of weeping*.
–

The video voice-over
tells *its* true-story? of

A king's soldiers, who shared
MacDonald hospitality.

A king's soldiers
with their signal to attack and kill.

And MacDonalds staining snow
with red and fleeing footprints

The voice-over tells
of the king's secretary of state,
Sir John Dalrymple of Stair
with orders for the massacre
signed by King William's own hand,
who ensured the MacDonalds of Glencoe
were made an example of
in spite of their *oath-of-loyalty* to the king.

The voice-over tells
of the captain of the king's forces,
Robert Campbell of Glen Lyon
who was the only Campbell there
teaching the unruly highlanders
the king's lesson.

—

and to cover up the facts
that the MacDonalds were butchered
on a blanket of early morning snow

Glencoe's myth was born
of yet another battle
between cattle-thieves and rebellious chiefs

as authentic as
the scene sold to present-day tourists
of kilted figures playing laments
at the entrance to the glen of weeping

as if every Scottish mountain
came complete with its own Scottish piper.

Nacho-Munchers
& Dolly-Grips

At the 14 screen *Mega-Multiplex*

They crunch the popcorn carpet
flashing torches
like a night at the blitz.
They seat chattering late-arrivals
for the summer's *must-see* block-
    buster.

A cellophane-crinkler's
mobile releases William Tell.

A big-gulp-slurper
advises the cellophane-crinkler –

'Yir no supposed tae hiv that oan!'

A nacho-muncher
advises the big-gulp-slurper –
'Away an gie's peace,
you're noisier than the fuckin
    phone.'

And the hero
who's saving America
and therefore, the world,
makes his first reel appearance.

At the *Art-house Cinema*

The volume of audience murmur
decreases in synchronisation
with the dimming houselights.

They settle down
getting seriously comfortable
draping legs over seats

in preparation to watch –

*The idiosyncratic, ironic
dramatisation;
the delicious fictional concoction,
that bristles with emotional
insight,
and drags the horror genre
away from its origins
by making its threat existential.*

And at the film's closing
when the credits roll,
a silent audience disapproval
permeates the atmosphere
if someone dares leave early.

So -- who are you when you go to see a film?
Are you a seasoned
cellophane-crinkling
ice-cream carton-scraping
big-gulp-slurping
hot-dog-chomping
nacho-muncher?

Or are you the one
that watches till the very end, for the dolly-grip roll-call,
satisfied you have done your duty?

Stopping Time

At 4:00 p.m. the boiler-makers
crowd clatty toilets.
They squirt jellied cleanser
on the black of their hands.

They nudge each other in the ribs
'Whit happened, did yi fa?'
Their standard *'dirty hands'* joke.

At 4:10 p.m. they fasten donkey jackets.

They edge past the oil-smell of machines
(as if executing an illicit jailbreak),
past the noise of shed-door rollers,
into daylight on the cobbled street
behind closed gates with barbed wire pelmets

joining *fitters*, *turners*, *joiners*,
plumbers, *sparks* and *labourers* and –

at 4:18 p.m.
the hooter's blast punctures the quiet.

The gates swing open
and the mass, flood out of the yard
like a full-time football crowd.

spilling into pubs, cars, trains, buses and clubs.

spilling into an escape that lasts

until next morning's 7:30 a.m. hooter
when they shuffle their return
like captured escapees
in a prisoner-of-war movie
full of tired old clichés.

I am the Dark

Late at night if you
open the bedroom door
I leak into the hall

If you go downstairs
I'll be there, waiting

If you peer from behind the curtains –

you'll find me
        out of reach of searching street-lights
you'll find me
        in the sky speckled with starry dreams
you'll find me
        inside the sleepy corners of your head.

I have many friends –

The reflections in puddles
that wobble like multi-coloured jellies
when you stamp-splash them.

The fireworks that explode
rainbow bursts
and drizzle dripping silver.

The night-time animals
that slumber daytime dreams
waiting for the sun to be tucked in by the moon.

and the wished-upon stars
that glimmer at their brightest
when I am at my blackest.

Forever

When someone tells you
they'll love you forever,
you should know it's a downright lie,
because forever is all the stuff that happens
long after the day that you die.

Flights of Imagination

Your imagination ... can flutter
like moths in darkness
searching for light.

... can glide
like flying-squirrels
leaping from tree to tree.

... can spin
like whirling sycamore seeds
propelled by a fresh breeze.

... can rise
like flying fish
who forgot they could only swim.

... can soar
like golden eagles
wheeling on whistling winds.

... can zoom
like whooshing rockets
spitting fire
as they shoot for the heavens.

Your imagination can
free the limits of your mind
with the infinity of your dreams.

Your imagination can fly ... if you let it.

Sandalwood

Our visiting footsteps
along the path of
The West Highland Way,
like us,
exploring new directions.

Underfoot, our city shoes
crack twigs, crunch leaves.

A distant lament
faintly stirs the air.
An unseen piper adding
the essential Scottish ingredient.

In a Loch Lomond bay
that could've
come from
an exotic calendar shoot,
we rest on the flatness
of rocks, warm in the sun.

Talking, probing,
laughing at nothing in particular.

A powerboat vroooooooms in the foreground,
Crows Craaaaaaw in the background,

a hover-plane buzzes overhead;
a speck in the bluest of sky.

Broken glass chips in the sand
sparkle
like diamonds
scattered absent-mindedly.

The fragrance of your *sandalwood*,
and you;
lingering in the
crisp freshness of autumn air.

Some other books published by **LUATH** PRESS

POETRY

Tartan & Turban
Bashabi Fraser
ISBN 1 84282 044 3 PB £8.99

The Ruba'iyat of Omar Khayyam, in Scots
Rab Wilson
ISBN 1 84282 046 X PB £8.99

Talking with Tongues
Brian D. Finch
ISBN 1 84282 006 0 PB £8.99

Kate o Shanter's Tale and other poems [book]
Matthew Fitt
ISBN 1 84282 028 1 PB £6.99

Kate o Shanter's Tale and other poems [audio CD]
Matthew Fitt
ISBN 1 84282 043 5 PB £9.99

Bad Ass Raindrop
Kokumo Rocks
ISBN 1 84282 018 4 PB £6.99

Madame Fifi's Farewell and other poems
Gerry Cambridge
ISBN 1 84282 005 2 PB £8.99

Poems to be Read Aloud
introduced by Tom Atkinson
ISBN 0 946487 00 6 PB £5.00

Scots Poems to be Read Aloud
introduced by Stuart McHardy
ISBN 0 946487 81 2 PB £5.00

Picking Brambles
Des Dillon
ISBN 1 84282 021 4 PB £6.99

Sex, Death & Football
Alistair Findlay
ISBN 1 84282 022 2 PB £6.99

The Luath Burns Companion
John Cairney
ISBN 1 84282 000 1 PB £10.00

Immortal Memories: A Compilation of Toasts to the Memory of Burns as delivered at Burns Suppers, 1801-2001
John Cairney
ISBN 1 84282 009 5 HB £20.00

The Whisky Muse: Scotch whisky in poem & song
Robin Laing
ISBN 1 84282 041 9 PB £7.99

FICTION

Driftnet
Lin Anderson
ISBN 1 84282 034 6 PB £9.99

The Fundamentals of New Caledonia
David Nicol
ISBN 1 84282 93 6 HB £16.99

Milk Treading
Nick Smith
ISBN 1 84282 037 0 PB £6.99

The Road Dance
John MacKay
ISBN 1 84282 024 9 PB £9.99

The Strange Case of RL Stevenson
Richard Woodhead
ISBN 0 946487 86 3 HB £16.99

But n Ben A-Go-Go
Matthew Fitt
ISBN 0 946487 82 0 HB £10.99
ISBN 1 84282 014 1 PB £6.99

The Bannockburn Years
William Scott
ISBN 0 946487 34 0 PB £7.95

Outlandish Affairs: An Anthology of Amorous Encounters
Edited and introduced by Evan Rosenthal and Amanda Robinson
ISBN 1 84282 055 9 PB £9.99

FOLKLORE

Scotland: Myth Legend & Folklore
Stuart McHardy
ISBN 0 946487 69 3 PB £7.99

The Supernatural Highlands
Francis Thompson
ISBN 0 946487 31 6 PB £8.99

Tall Tales from an Island
Peter Macnab
ISBN 0 946487 07 3 PB £8.99

Tales from the North Coast
Alan Temperley
ISBN 0 946487 18 9 PB £8.99

THE QUEST FOR

The Quest for Robert Louis Stevenson
John Cairney
ISBN 0 946487 87 1 HB £16.99

The Quest for the Nine Maidens
Stuart McHardy
ISBN 0 946487 66 9 HB £16.99

The Quest for the Original Horse Whisperers
Russell Lyon
ISBN 1 842820 020 6 HB £16.99

The Quest for the Celtic Key
Karen Ralls-MacLeod and
Ian Robertson
ISBN 1 842820 031 1 PB £8.99

The Quest for Arthur
Stuart McHardy
ISBN 1 842820 12 5 HB £16.99

ON THE TRAIL OF

On the Trail of John Muir
Cherry Good
ISBN 0 946487 62 6 PB £7.99

On the Trail of Mary Queen of Scots
J. Keith Cheetham
ISBN 0 946487 50 2 PB £7.99

On the Trail of William Wallace
David R. Ross
ISBN 0 946487 47 2 PB £7.99

On the Trail of Robert Burns
John Cairney
ISBN 0 946487 51 0 PB £7.99

On the Trail of Bonnie Prince Charlie
David R. Ross
ISBN 0 946487 68 5 PB £7.99

On the Trail of Queen Victoria in the Highlands
Ian R. Mitchell
ISBN 0 946487 79 0 PB £7.99

On the Trail of Robert the Bruce
David R. Ross
ISBN 0 946487 52 9 PB £7.99

On the Trail of Robert Service
GW Lockhart
ISBN 0 946487 24 3 PB £7.99

LANGUAGE

Luath Scots Language Learner [Book]
L Colin Wilson
ISBN 0 946487 91 X PB £9.99

Luath Scots Language Learner [Double Audio CD Set]
L Colin Wilson
ISBN 1 84282 026 5 CD £16.99

WALK WITH LUATH

Mountain Days & Bothy Nights
Dave Brown and Ian Mitchell
ISBN 0 946487 15 4 PB £7.50

The Joy of Hillwalking
Ralph Storer
ISBN 0 946487 28 6 PB £7.50

Scotland's Mountains before the Mountaineers
Ian R Mitchell
ISBN 0 946487 39 1 PB £9.99

Mountain Outlaw
Ian R Mitchell
ISBN 1 84282 027 3 PB £6.50

NEW SCOTLAND

Some Assembly Required: behind the scenes at the rebirth of the Scottish Parliament
Andy Wightman
ISBN 0 946487 84 7 PB £7.99

Scotland - Land and Power the agenda for land reform
Andy Wightman
ISBN 0 946487 70 7 PB £5.00

Old Scotland New Scotland
Jeff Fallow
ISBN 0 946487 40 5 PB £6.99

Notes from the North Incorporating a Brief History of the Scots and the English
Emma Wood
ISBN 0 946487 46 4 PB £8.99

Scotlands of the Future: sustainability in a small nation
Edited by Eurig Scandrett
ISBN 1 84282 035 4 PB £7.99

Eurovision or American Dream? Britain, the Euro and the future of Europe
David Purdy
ISBN 1 84282 036 2 PB £3.99

HISTORY

Reportage Scotland: History in the Making
Louise Yeoman
ISBN 0 946487 61 8 PB £9.99

Edinburgh's Historic Mile
Duncan Priddle
ISBN 0 946487 97 9 PB £2.99

A Passion for Scotland
David R Ross
ISBN 1 84282 019 2 PB £5.99

Scots in Canada
Jenni Calder
ISBN 1 84282 038 9 PB £7.99

Plaids & Bandanas: Highland Drover to Wild West Cowboy
Rob Gibson
ISBN 0 946487 88 X PB £7.99

SOCIAL HISTORY

Shale Voices
Alistair Findlay
foreword by Tam Dalyell MP
ISBN 0 946487 63 4 PB £10.99
ISBN 0 946487 78 2 HB £17.99

Crofting Years
Francis Thompson
ISBN 0 946487 06 5 PB £6.95

A Word for Scotland
Jack Campbell
foreword by Magnus Magnusson
ISBN 0 946487 48 0 PB £12.99

Luath Press Limited
committed to publishing well written books worth reading

LUATH PRESS takes its name from Robert Burns, whose little collie Luath (*Gael.*, swift or nimble) tripped up Jean Armour at a wedding and gave him the chance to speak to the woman who was to be his wife and the abiding love of his life. Burns called one of *The Twa Dogs* Luath after Cuchullin's hunting dog in *Ossian's Fingal*. Luath Press was established in 1981 in the heart of Burns country, and is now based a few steps up the road from Burns' first lodgings on Edinburgh's Royal Mile.
Luath offers you distinctive writing with a hint of unexpected pleasures.

Most bookshops in the UK, the US, Canada, Australia, New Zealand and parts of Europe either carry our books in stock or can order them for you. To order direct from us, please send a £sterling cheque, postal order, international money order or your credit card details (number, address of cardholder and expiry date) to us at the address below. Please add post and packing as follows:
UK – £1.00 per delivery address; overseas surface mail – £2.50 per delivery address; overseas airmail – £3.50 for the first book to each delivery address, plus £1.00 for each additional book by airmail to the same address. If your order is a gift, we will happily enclose your card or message at no extra charge.

Luath Press Limited
543/2 Castlehill
The Royal Mile
Edinburgh EH1 2ND
Scotland
Telephone: 0131 225 4326 (24 hours)
Fax: 0131 225 4324
email: gavin.macdougall@luath.co.uk
Website: www.luath.co.uk